W9-AVR-384

Easy
BBQ
Sauces, Rubs, Mops, Marinades and More!

**GOLDEN
WEST** ☼
PUBLISHERS

ISBN 13: 978-1-58581-023-9
ISBN 10: 1-58581-023-1

Printed in the United States of America
1st printing © 2007

Copyright © 2006 Golden West Publishers. All rights reserved. This book or any portion thereof, may not be reproduced in any form, except for review purposes, without the written permission of the publisher.

Information in this book is deemed to be authentic and accurate by authors and publisher. However, they disclaim any liability incurred in connection with the use of information appearing in this book.

Illustrations: Sean Hoy
Interior Design: The Printed Page

Golden West Publishers
4113 N. Longview
Phoenix, AZ 85014
(800) 658-5830

For free sample recipes from every Golden West cookbook, visit:
www.goldenwestpublishers.com

Foreword

Meet BBQ Joe Hartmann, the all-around American family man, who loves his family, friends, good times and, last but not least, his mad passion for his barbecue get-togethers!

Anyone invited to Joe's for barbecue knows it's down to the basics—good company, comfortable surroundings and the best barbecue in the county—just ask all who know.

Summer picnics, football and basketball parties, reunions, holidays or just a Sunday kickback are all reasons to join the gang at Joe's. All "gang members" impatiently wait to receive that special invitation to meet at Joe's place.

Who is Joe? He is the spirit of all Americans getting back to the basics. He is the Primal American, not lost, but rejuvenated; smoke, meat, fire, wood, stimulating our senses and pleasures, maybe born from ancient times. We all know the primal pleasure in that heavenly smell as we gather round the pit, smoker or grill to socialize.

This book is a culmination of years of collecting, experimenting, cooking and playing. It's all here for your next barbecue. You can be BBQ Joe, John, Tom, Dick or Jane. Start with your favorite sauce and make it your own. Or follow the recipe to a "T."

Either way, you will be the hit of the party. Remember, the secret to a great barbecue is in the Sauce!

Contents

Introduction

As the story goes, the Southern custom of barbecue originated in the state of Virginia before the 1700s.

Yet, the term barbecue became popular with the advent of the Western Cowboy in the 1800s. Cattle drive herd owners were not keen on feeding the cowboys good cuts of meat, so beef brisket was the order of the day. Beef brisket had a reputation for being tough and stringy. Basically, the meat had no redeeming appetizing appeal at all!

Yet, the cowboys persevered. They soon discovered a method for making the brisket tender. They cooked the meat for a long period of time—usually 5-7 hours at a low temperature of 200 degrees or thereabouts—and basted often during the cooking process.

The result was incredible, mouth-watering, tender, succulent meat. Soon other meats such as beef ribs, venison, pork and goat were added to the blend. Thus the new cooking method became the popular barbecue we love today!

Add to this social culture the secret sauces, slow cooking and cold beer, and you have a phenomenon that grows each year. Yes, we love our barbecue!

Let's look at a few methods used to make that special barbecue successful.

Baste: When you pick your sauce, think about the people you are pleasing. Sauces are flavor-enhancing and satisfy our taste buds. Grilled cuts such as chops and ribs are ideal. You can take  your favorite bottled sauce and add a secret ingredient or two to enhance and make it your own. Flavor boosters such as chile pepper/chili powder, and even an orange marmalade can individualize any store-bought sauce!

Apply your sauce to beef, pork, seafood or poultry and you have a baste. But, if you are brushing your baste from the container, please be sure to put it back in the pan and heat to a low boil for 30 seconds to prevent meat contamination. This is a great way to combine old flavors with new. You can replenish your stock, mix it and boil it, and refrigerate. Each time you add to the baste, you are adding new flavors and eventually you will create something quite different from the original, unique and irresistible.

Dry Rub: A dry mixture that is store-bought or homemade is an endless option to spice up your food such as pork and beef tenderloin, chops and ribs. Herbs and spices will add delicious flavors without the fat. Herbs with bold flavors such as rosemary, cumin, coriander, and cayenne work well as rubs. When they combine with the natural juices of the meats they work as a "dry" marinade.

Hand rub the mixture onto the meat the night before or just before cooking to boost the flavor and intensity. You can decide if a little or large amount will suit you.

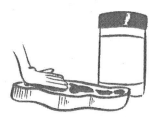

Mop: Mops add flavor and moisture to any beef, pork, poultry or seafood while cooking. Mops tend to be thin and watery. They contain spices but usually no sugar or tomatoes. Sugar can caramelize over the open fire and burn the meat. A mop head utensil, usually cotton-tipped to allow for a generous application, can be utilized during the mopping process.

Some barbecue aficionados take claim that a mop is nothing more than a smoking sauce. One can use a mop that contains sugar if smoking at a temperature below 265 degrees. However, if grilling, sugar should be avoided all together to avoid burning.

Marinade: Soak raw meats in a marinade to make them tastier, juicier and even healthier! Marinades contain flavorings, herbs, spices, vinegars or other acidic liquids and oil. The oil holds in the moisture by reducing loss during cooking. Being acidic, the  marinade carries seasoning flavors into the meats. The acidic nature also protects the meat from harmful substances during grilling on the open fire.

Keep food covered in the refrigerator when marinating. If you wish to use the marinade for basting, reserve a portion to use later. It is advised not to reuse marinades in which raw food has soaked.

Barbecue

When referring to the term "barbecue," which has an acceptable spelling of "barbeque," one can refer to either the meat itself (which is the noun) or the act of barbecuing (a verb).

Once we thought of barbecue as a predominately a Southern dish, yet today we acknowledge many regional differences.

Texans loves their smoked brisket. Pork is king in Tennessee. Aficionados blend spices and herbs to create their rubs, and South Carolina has a corner market on mustard rubs. Looking to the north, neighboring North Carolina takes the lead with vinegar-based meat.

Well, that's the way some people see it.

But most will agree, when it comes to barbecuing, chefs take great pride in creating their own phenomenal sauces that are generally guarded as their "secret recipes."

Easy BBQ Sauces, Rubs, Mops, Marinades and More! provides an array of sauces, etc. to make your own mouthwatering, barbecue "secret recipe." We urge you to embellish upon our offerings or make your own from scratch. Either way, enjoy the quest!

Hints from BBQ Experts:

* When lighting a gas grill, always keep the lid open.

* Position your grill in an open area away from high traffic spots or buildings.

* Check the propane level in the tank before you begin to grill.

* When you grill, do not wear clothing that has a hanging shirt tail or apron string.

* Marinate your food ahead of time and in the refrigerator, never on the counter.

Hints from BBQ Experts:

❖ When grilling fruit or vegetables, place them on the outer edge of the grill to keep from burning.

❖ To help prevent burns or spatters, always use long handled utensils.

❖ You can minimize loss of juice if you use a spatula or tongs to pick up meat, etc. instead of a fork.

❖ Cook your meat thoroughly by checking a meat or "instant read" thermometer. Poultry is generally cooked to 180 degrees and a chicken breast to 170 degrees F. Beef, lamb, veal roasts/steaks are cooked to 145 degrees to 160 degrees and burgers and pork should be cooked to 160 degrees.

Did You Know?

❖ The number one grilling favorite is hamburger, followed by steak, chicken and then hot dogs.

❖ Corn is the most commonly prepared vegetable on the grill.

❖ The most popular variety of sauce is hickory-flavored, then mesquite and third is honey.

❖ To gauge the temperature of the charcoal fire, carefully hold out your hand, palm side down, just above the cooking grill. If you can keep it there for five seconds, the temperature is low. Four seconds is medium heat, three seconds is medium-hot and finally, one to two seconds is hot.

❖ Aluminum foil is known as the most popular helper "utensil" and is used in the preparation of side dishes.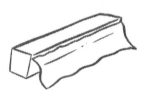

Easy BBQ Tips

(not in order)

Charcoal Tips

❖ When your coals begin to gray and show signs of ruby red, place your meat, chicken or fish on the grill. Place the meat side-by-side and touching so you cover the entire rack. Any gaps will result in drawing off the heat; so be careful how you place items on the grill.

❖ Always keep a small bottle of water near your BBQ. When you do spray to control problems, remember to spray only the meat and whatever is causing the fire. You want to maintain the heat that you have developed.

❖ After you make your one and only turn of the meat, place a few water-soaked mesquite chips on the grill. The rising smoke from the chips will enhance the flavor of the meat.

❖ When you use your grill for the first time, or after a very good scrubbing, brush the grill grate with olive oil. This will attract certain flavors to enhance the flavor of everything you cook as well as help keep your meat from sticking to the grill.

❖ To have successful fire in a grill, use enough charcoal briquettes to cover the actual grilling area. Stack the briquettes in a pyramid fashion so they light faster and keep the air circulating around the food.

Safety Tips

❖ Always read your owner's manual first before using your grill.

❖ Use your LP gas canisters carefully. Always give them good ventilation. Make sure the lid is open when lighting the burners.

❖ If you smell gas and your attempt to light it fails, turn off the burners and wait five minutes before attempting to light it again.

❖ Don't use grills on wooden porches, balconies or beneath overhangs. The heat could cause a ceiling fire. Keep a water bottle and fire extinguisher nearby.

❖ Be sure that your grill is on an even surface to avoid tipping.

❖ Don't leave your grill unattended for more than a few minutes and never leave it if children are nearby. Be careful when pets are around, too.

❖ Turn off the LP gas cylinder valve after each use.

Sauces

Rib Sauce

1 cup **Tomato Sauce**
1 cup **Vinegar**
1 cup **Water**
2 tsp. **Salt**
1 tbsp. **Butter**
1 tsp. **Honey**
Dash of **Pepper**

Combine all ingredients in a saucepan and mix thoroughly. Bring to a boil, then simmer for 15 minutes. Place in a bowl, cover and cool for several hours until thickened.

Three-Alarm Sauce

1 tbsp. **Onion Flakes**
1 tbsp. **Salt**
3 tsp. **Hot Pepper Sauce**
3 tsp. **Sugar**
1 pint **Cider Vinegar**

Combine all ingredients in a mixing bowl, pouring in the vinegar last. Mix well. Let stand 3 hours.

Sweet Sauce

2 cups **Ketchup**
2 cups **Sugar**
1/2 cup **Water**
1 cup **Lemon Juice**
3 tsp. **Butter**
2 tsp. **Molasses**
1 tsp. **Honey**
1 tsp. **Hot Sauce**
1 tsp. **Steak Sauce**

Combine all ingredients in a saucepan and mix thoroughly. Bring to a boil, then simmer for 15 minutes. Place in a bowl, cover and let cool for several hours until thickened.

Golden Grill Barbecue Sauce

1/4 cup **Sugar**
2 tbsp. **Cornstarch**
1/2 tsp. **Allspice**
1/2 tsp. ground **Cloves**
1 cup fresh **Orange Juice**
2 tbsp. **Vinegar**
4 tbsp. **Butter** or **Margarine**

Combine sugar, cornstarch, allspice and cloves in a small saucepan. Slowly stir in orange juice and vinegar. Stir constantly over medium heat until sauce thickens. Boil for 3 minutes. Stir in butter. Makes 1 cup sauce.

Bob's Barbecue Sauce

1 cup **Ketchup**
1/2 cup **Cider Vinegar**
1 tsp. **Sugar**
1 tsp. **Chili Powder**
1/8 tsp. **Salt**
1 1/2 cups **Water**
3 stalks **Celery**, chopped
3 **Bay Leaves**
1 clove **Garlic**
2 tbsp. chopped **Onion**
4 tbsp. **Butter**
4 tbsp. **Worcestershire Sauce**
1 tsp. **Paprika**
Dash **Black Pepper**

Combine all ingredients and bring to a boil. Simmer about 15 minutes. Remove from heat and strain. This is a table sauce to be served with beef, chicken or pork. Do not cook things in it. Makes about 2 1/2 cups sauce.

Bob's

Pioneer Bar-B-Que Sauce

3 tbsp. **Margarine**
1/2 cup diced **Onions**
1 cup **Tomato Puree**
3 tbsp. **Worcestershire Sauce**
1 1/3 cups **Ketchup**
3 tbsp. **Steak Sauce**
1 tbsp. **Vinegar**
1 tsp. **Lemon Juice**
2 tbsp. **Liquid Smoke**
1 1/2 tsp. **Soy Sauce**
3/4 tsp. **Dry Mustard**
2 tbsp. **Honey**
2 tbsp. **Brown Sugar**
1 tsp. **Accent**®
1 1/2 tsp. **Salt**
1/2 to 1 tsp. **Chili Powder**
4 cups **Hot Water**
Scant **Black Pepper**

Melt margarine and sauté onions. Add remaining ingredients and mix. Simmer one hour or longer until sauce is of desired consistency. Sauce may be frozen at this point. Makes 6 cups.

Note: To thicken sauce quickly, add 2 tbsp. cornstarch to 2 cups cold water. Add to sauce and cook until sauce thickens. Do not freeze after cornstarch has been added.

Spicy Tomato Sauce

1 cup **Spicy Tomato Juice**
1/3 cup **Hoisin Sauce**
3 tbsp. **Orange Juice**
2 tbsp. **Water**
1 tsp. **Olive Oil**
1 tsp. **Lemon Juice**
1 tsp. chopped **Onion**

Combine all ingredients in a saucepan and mix thoroughly. Bring to a boil, then simmer for 15 minutes. Place in a bowl, cover and cool for several hours until thickened.

Refrigerator Door Sauce

12 oz. **Ketchup**
1/4 cup **Honey**
1/4 cup **Mustard**
2 tsp. **Sherry Vinegar**
2 tbsp. **Water**
1 tbsp. **Worcestershire Sauce**
1 tsp. **Olive Oil**

Combine all ingredients in a saucepan and mix thoroughly. Bring to a boil, then simmer for 15 minutes. Place in a bowl, cover and let cool for several hours until thickened.

Brown Sugar Barbecue Sauce

1/4 cup **Butter**
1 tbsp. **Flour**
1 clove **Garlic**, minced
2 cups **Tomato Juice**
3 tbsp. **Lemon Juice**
1 tbsp. **Worcestershire Sauce**
2 tbsp. **Brown Sugar**
1 tsp. **Dry Mustard**
1 tsp. **Chili Powder**
1 tsp. **Salt**
1/3 cup chopped **Black Olives**
1/4 cup chopped **Onion**

Melt butter; stir in flour and garlic. Add tomato juice. Cook and stir a few minutes. Mix in remaining ingredients except olives and simmer 15 minutes. Add olives to sauce. Simmer five minutes. Use to baste barbecued meats, poultry, or fish. Makes about 2 cups.

Grandma's Old Fashioned BBQ Sauce

1 bottle (8 oz.) **Cooking Oil**
6 large **Onions,** diced
6 cans (8 oz.) **Tomato Sauce**
1 stick, 1/4 lb. **Butter**
2 tsp. **Prepared Mustard**
1 1/2 tbsp. **Mayonnaise**
1 bottle (14 oz.) **Ketchup**
25-30 drops **Tabasco® Sauce**
3 cups **Sugar**

Heat cooking oil. Stir in onions and cook to soften. Add tomato sauce; let simmer three minutes. Add remaining ingredients, except sugar, and cook five minutes. Gradually add sugar, stirring constantly. Lower heat, cover and cook slowly about 1-2 hours. Sauce can be used over spaghetti.

Although some parts of the country, when barbecuing meat on an outdoor grill rotisserie or pit, use such woods as hickory or oak, most of Texas and the Southwestern United States use mesquite (mes-keet). Mesquite, a small native desert tree, grows wild in the desert and chaparral areas of the Southwest and Mexico. Burning aromatic mesquite logs or charcoal produces a smoke that lends a distinctive and appetizing flavor to beef, ribs and varieties of meat, fish, poultry and vegetables.

Lubbock's Favorite BBQ Sauce

2 tbsp. **Oil**
1 **Onion**, chopped
1 cup **Ketchup**
1/2 cup **Water**
1/4 cup **Brown Sugar**
3 tbsp. **Worcestershire Sauce**
1 tbsp. **Salt**
1/4 tsp. **Garlic Powder**

Heat oil in saucepan and sauté onion until tender. Add remaining ingredients, stir and simmer covered for about 8-10 minutes. Makes 2 cups sauce.

Lubbock, in the South Plains region is one of the main agricultural centers of Texas. The city ships livestock, grain and cotton. It was named for Col. Thomas Lubbock, a Confederate officer and brother of a Texas governor.

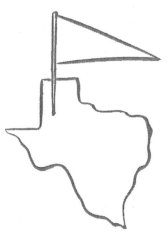

Barbecue Sauce with Mushrooms

1/4 cup **Oil**
3/4 cup minced **Onion**
3/4 cup minced **Celery**
1/2 cup minced **Mushrooms**
1/2 cup **Brown Sugar**
1 tbsp. plus 1 tsp. **Prepared Mustard**
1 tsp. **Salt**
1 tbsp. plus 1 tsp. **Worcestershire Sauce**
2 tbsp. **Cider Vinegar**
1 1/4 cups **Water**

Heat oil in a saucepan. Add minced vegetables and sauté without browning. Add remaining ingredients, stir and simmer for 30 minutes. Stir occasionally or until thickened. Makes 1 quart of sauce.

Ranch Barbecue Sauce

1/3 cup **Dill Pickle Juice**
1/3 cup **Chili Sauce**
2 tsp. **Worcestershire Sauce**
1/2 tsp. **Salt**
3 tbsp. diced **Dill Pickle**
2 drops **Tabasco**® **Sauce**

Mix all ingredients together and serve with your favorite meat fish or poultry.

Mom Mac's BBQ Sauce

The Phoenix Gazette

1 can (8-oz.) **Tomato Sauce** (or 1 cup **Ketchup**)
1 can (or 1 cup) **Water**
2 tbsp. **Brown Sugar**
2 tbsp. **Vinegar**
2 tbsp. **Worcestershire Sauce**
2 **Onions**, sliced
1 tsp. **Salt**
1/4 tsp. **Pepper**
1 tsp. (or more) **Paprika**
Dash **Cayenne Pepper**
Liquid Hickory Smoke Flavoring (optional)

Combine all ingredients in saucepan. Simmer for 5-8 minutes, then brush on meat of choice.

Wine BBQ Base

1/2 cup **California Burgundy**
1/2 cup **Chili Sauce**
1/4 cup **Water** or **Broth**
1 tbsp. grated **Onion**
1 tbsp. **Worcestershire Sauce**
Dash **Garlic Powder**

Combine ingredients and simmer together for 5 minutes.
Use this sauce to baste meat on barbecue grill or broiler.

Spicy Steak Sauce

Barbecue Industry Association

1 cup **Ketchup**
1/2 cup **Water**
1/4 cup **Soy Sauce**
2 tbsp. **Vinegar**
1 tbsp. **Brown Sugar**
1 tsp. **Prepared Mustard**
1 tsp. **Prepared Horseradish**
1 clove **Garlic**, crushed

In small saucepan, combine catsup, water, soy sauce, vinegar,
brown sugar, mustard, horseradish and garlic. Simmer for 10
to 15 minutes on back of grill.

Tip: Before barbecuing, slash through fat on the outside of
steaks at one-inch intervals to prevent curling.

Jane's Barbecue Sauce

Jane Kolb, Frisco, Texas

3/4 cup **Cider Vinegar**
3/4 cup **Water**
1 cup **Ketchup**
1 tbsp. **Salt**
1/2 cup **Chili Sauce**
1 tsp. **Pepper**
1 tsp. **Paprika**
6 tbsp. **Worcestershire Sauce**
2 tbsp. **Dark Brown Sugar**
2 tbsp. minced **Onion**
1 tbsp. **Molasses**
1 cup **Butter**
3 tbsp. **Dry Mustard**

Combine all ingredients and simmer until thickened.

Johnnie's BBQ Basting Sauce

1/2 tsp. **Salt**
1 tsp. **Dry Mustard**
1 clove **Garlic**, crushed
1/2 small **Bay Leaf**
1/3 tsp. **Chili Powder**
1/2 tsp. **Paprika**
3/4 tsp. **Hot Pepper Sauce**
1/2 cup **Worcestershire Sauce**
1/4 cup **Cider Vinegar**
2 cups **Beef Stock** (or canned beef bouillon)
1/4 cup **Vegetable Oil**

Combine all ingredients. Grill ribs slowly, basting often with sauce. (This sauce will keep several days in refrigerator and can be frozen.) If ribs are cut into serving pieces, the sauce will baste eight pounds of ribs.

Tip: Line the grill firebox with heavy-duty aluminum foil and about an inch of gravel. The gravel acts as an insulator to keep the fire hotter.

Lemon Bar-B-Q Sauce for Fish

Josephine S. Young, Gardena, California

1/2 cup **Lemon Juice**
1/4 cup **Salad Oil**
2 tbsp. grated **Onion**
1/2 tsp. **Salt**
1/2 tsp. **Black Pepper**
1 tsp. **Dry Mustard**
2 tbsp. **Brown Sugar**
Dash of **Tabasco® Sauce**

Mix ingredients well, stirring until sugar is dissolved. (Makes enough sauce for one pound fish fillets.)

Yellow Mustard Sauce

1 cup **Yellow Mustard**
1 cup **Red Wine Vinegar**
1/4 cup **Sugar**
1 1/2 tbsp. **Butter**
2 tsp. **Salt**
1 tsp. **Worcestershire Sauce**
1 1/4 tsp. ground **Black Pepper**
1/2 tsp. **Tabasco® Sauce**

In a medium saucepan, combine all ingredients. Stir until blended. Simmer 30 minutes on low heat. Let stand at room temperature 1 hour before using.

Aunt Polly's Barbecue Sauce

Courtesy Susan Nunn, Tempe, Arizona

1 can (28 oz.) **Tomatoes**
2 large **Onions**, chopped
5 oz. **Worcestershire Sauce**
1 can (15 1/2 oz.) **Crushed Pineapple**, drained
1/2 cup (or more) **Molasses** or **Honey**, to taste
Fresh **Ground Pepper**, to taste
1 bottle (28 oz.) **Hickory-Flavored Barbecue Sauce**

In crockery slow cooker, combine ingredients, (except for Barbecue Sauce) breaking up canned Tomatoes with a spoon. Add bottled barbecue sauce and simmer for about five hours.

Recaito Sauce
a la Goya

Original recipe created by Master Chef Felipe Rojas Lombardi expressly for the Goya Foods, Inc. Latin Barbecue a la Goya Cookbook. All rights reserved.

1/2 cup **Goya**® **Extra-Virgin Spanish Olive Oil**
2 large cloves **Garlic**, finely minced
1 cup finely chopped **Onion**
2 tbsp. finely chopped fresh **Ginger**
2 tbsp. **Goya**® **Hot Sauce**
4 tbsp. **Goya**® **Recaito**
1/4 cup **Water**
2 tbsp. **Lemon Juice**
1/4 tsp. **White Pepper**
1 tsp. **Sugar**
1/2 cup finely chopped **Coriander Leaves (Cilantro)**
1/2 cup **La Vina White Cooking Wine**

Heat oil in saucepan, saute garlic and ginger until golden. Add onions and saute until translucent. Stir in other ingredients and simmer ten minutes. This is salsa for fish. Makes two cups.

Note: Goya® Recaito is a puree of fresh green peppers, onions, garlic and fresh Coriander, an authentic spice and condiment mixture distinctively Latin in taste.

Basting Sauce for Venison

1 cup **Red Wine**
2/3 cup **Cider Vinegar**
Juice from **2 Limes** (or **2 lemons**)
3 cups **Hot Water**
1 stick **Butter** (or **Margarine**)
2 cloves **Garlic**, pressed
1 tbsp. **Salt**
2 tbsp. **Pepper**

Combine all ingredients in saucepan, mix well and heat.

Place meat on grill over low charcoal fire and baste with sauce every 15 to 20 minutes. Keep sauce hot while basting and stir sauce frequently. Cook until meat is tender, about four or five hours. Serves 8 to 10.

Carolina Style Sauce

1 1/2 cups **Distilled White** (or **Cider**) **Vinegar**
10 tbsp. **Ketchup**
Salt, to taste
Freshly ground **Pepper**, to taste
1/2 tsp. **Cayenne Pepper**
Pinch of crushed **Hot Red Pepper Flakes**
1 tbsp. **Sugar**
1/2 cup **Water**

Combine all ingredients in a small saucepan and bring to a simmer. Simmer and stir until the sugar dissolves. Remove from heat and let stand until cool. Serve on the side with barbecued meats. Makes 3 cups.

Chinese Barbecue For Fish

Li-Chen Hillhouse—Live Oak, Florida

12 oz. **Tomato Paste**
1 medium **Onion**, finely chopped
1 clove **Garlic**
1/4 cup **Soy Sauce**
8 to 10 drops **Tabasco**® **Sauce**
2 tbsp. **Butter**
Dash **Black Pepper**
1/2 cup **Cooking Oil**

Combine ingredients in small saucepan over low heat. DO NOT BOIL.

Whiskey Sauce for Fruit Kabobs

Courtesy The Kingsford Company

2 tbsp. **Honey**
2 tbsp. **Whiskey**
1 tbsp. **Lemon Juice**
1 can (8-oz.) **Pineapple Chunks,** drained
1 large **Banana,** bias sliced into 1-inch pieces
1 **Orange,** peeled and sectioned
8 **Maraschino Cherries**
4 **Skewers,** 12-inch, bamboo or metal

In a mixing bowl combine the honey, whiskey and lemon juice. Add pineapple chunks, banana pieces, orange sections and cherries. Gently toss to coat fruit well. Cover and refrigerate up to 2 hours until ready to grill. Remove fruit with slotted spoon, reserving the whiskey baste to brush on fruit kabobs while grilling.

Alternately thread the fruit onto skewers. Grill the fruit kabobs on a covered grill, directly over moderately low Kingsford® briquets for 5-10 minutes or until fruit is warmed through. Serves 4.

Note: If bamboo skewers are used, soak them in water for 20 minutes before using on the grill.

Pork Barbecue Basting Sauce

1 tsp. **Brown Sugar**
1 tbsp. **Paprika**
1 tsp. **Hickory Smoked Salt**
1 tsp. **Dry Mustard**
1/2 tsp. **Chili Powder**
1/8 tsp. **Cayenne Pepper**
2 tbsp. **Worcestershire Sauce**
1/4 cup **Vinegar**
1 cup **Tomato Sauce**
1/4 cup **Ketchup**
1/2 cup **Water**
Dash **Red Pepper**
Dash **Tabasco**® **Sauce**
1 **Bay Leaf**
2 cloves **Garlic**
1/8 tsp. **Lemon Juice**

Combine all ingredients and simmer for 15 minutes. Remove bay leaf and garlic cloves before basting pork.

Honey Spiced Barbecue Sauce

1 1/4 cups **Ketchup**
2/3 cup **Salad Oil**
3/4 cup **Vinegar** or **Red Wine**
5 tbsp. **Worcestershire Sauce**
1 cup **Honey**
2 tbsp. **Dry Mustard**
3 tsp. fresh grated **Ginger**
1 **Lemon**, sliced thin
3 tbsp. **Butter**

Combine all ingredients in a saucepan and heat to blend together. Makes enough sauce for four pounds of hamburger meat.

Lemon-Molasses Barbecue Sauce

1 bottle (18 oz.) **Barbecue Sauce**
1/2 cup **Brown Sugar**
2 tsp. **Lemon Juice**
2/3 cup diced **Onion**
1/4 cup **Molasses**
2 tsp. **Sweet Hot Mustard**

Combine all ingredients and boil until thick, stirring constantly. Makes 2 cups sauce.

Country-Style BBQ Sauce

1 cup **Ketchup**
1/2 cup **Cider Vinegar**
1 tsp. **Sugar**
1 tsp. **Chili Powder**
1/8 tsp. **Salt**
1 1/2 cups **Water**
3 stalks **Celery**, chopped
3 tbsp. chopped **Onion**
4 tbsp. **Butter**
4 tbsp. **Worcestershire Sauce**
1 tsp. **Paprika**
Dash of **Black Pepper**

Combine all ingredients and bring to a boil. Simmer about 15 minutes. Remove from heat and strain. Serve on the side with beef, chicken or pork. Makes 2 1/2 cups.

Poultry Barbecue Sauce

1/2 cup **Vegetable Oil**
1/4 cup **Vinegar**
1/4 cup **Worcestershire Sauce**
1 can (8 oz.) **Tomato Sauce**
2 1/2 tbsp. minced **Onion**
2 tbsp. **Brown Sugar**
1 tbsp. **Chili Powder**
1 tsp. **Sugar**
1/2 tsp. **Seasoned Salt**

Combine all ingredients and let stand for at least five minutes. Stir before using to brush on chicken or turkey parts or serve on the side. Makes 2 cups.

Western Barbecue Sauce

1 cup **Ketchup**
1 cup **Brown Sugar**
1/2 cup **Lemon Juice**
1/2 stick **Butter**
1/4 cup minced **Onion**
1 tsp. **Hot Pepper Sauce**
1 tsp. **Worcestershire Sauce**

Place all ingredients in a heavy saucepan and bring to a boil. Reduce heat and simmer for 30 minutes. Serve hot or cool; refrigerate in glass jars or bowls. Makes 3 cups.

Spicy Poultry Basting Sauce

1 cup **Orange Juice**
1/2 cup **Lemon Juice**
1/2 tsp. **Ginger Powder**
1/4 cup **Brown Sugar**

1 tsp. **Curry Powder**
1 tsp. **Black Pepper**
1/4 cup **Soy Sauce**
1/4 tsp. **Mace**

Combine all ingredients thoroughly. Baste turkey or chicken during last 30 minutes of cooking. Makes 2 cups sauce.

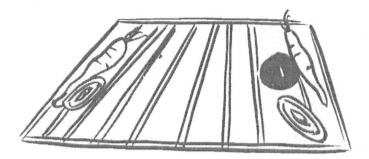

Low-Cal
Barbecue Sauce

1 cup fresh **Lemon Juice**
2/3 cup **Apple Cider Vinegar**
2/3 cup unsalted **Tomato Juice**
1/2 cup **Water**
3 tbsp. low-cal **Brown Sugar**
2 tsp. **Garlic Powder**
2 tsp. **Dry Mustard**
2 tsp. **Paprika**
1 tsp. ground **Black Pepper**
1 tsp. ground **Red Pepper**
1 tsp. pure **Onion Powder**
2 tsp. **Red Hot Sauce**
1/4 cup **Safflower Oil**

Combine all ingredients in a saucepan. Heat to boiling. Remove from heat and baste meat or poultry. Makes 3 cups.

Favorite Barbecue Sauce

1/2 cup **Oil**
1/2 cup finely chopped **Onion**
1/2 cup finely chopped **Celery**
1/2 cup finely chopped **Green Bell Pepper**
1 clove **Garlic**
2 tbsp. **Worcestershire Sauce**
3 tbsp. **Brown Sugar**
1 tsp. **Salt**
1 cup **Ketchup**
1/2 cup **Vinegar**
1/4 tsp. **Chili Powder**
2 tsp. **Dry Mustard**
2 tsp. prepared **Horseradish**
Juice of 1 **Lemon**

Combine all ingredients, heat and simmer covered until all vegetables are tender. Makes enough sauce to baste 4 chickens or a dozen hamburgers.

Sunday Special Sauce

1 cup **Ketchup**
1/2 cup **Cider Vinegar**
1 tsp. **Sugar**
1 tsp. **Chili Powder**
1/8 tsp. **Salt**
1 1/2 cups **Water**
3 stalks **Celery**, chopped
3 **Bay Leaves**
1 clove **Garlic**
2 tbsp. diced **Onion**
4 tbsp. **Butter**
4 tbsp. **Worcestershire Sauce**
1 tsp. **Paprika**
Pinch **Black Pepper**

Combine all ingredients in a saucepan and bring to a boil. Reduce heat and simmer 15 minutes. Remove from heat and strain. Place in glass bowl and refrigerate up to two weeks. Makes 2 1/2 cups sauce.

Sizzling Citrus Barbecue Sauce

1 tbsp. **Vegetable Oil**
1 medium **Onion**, chopped
1 tbsp. ground **Red Chiles**
1/4 tsp. ground **Red Pepper**
1 cup **Orange Juice**
1/2 cup **Lime Juice**
2 tbsp. **Sugar**
2 tbsp. **Lemon Juice**
1 tbsp. snipped fresh **Cilantro**
1 tsp. **Salt**

Place oil in pan. Add onion, ground red chiles, red pepper and heat, stirring frequently, until onion is translucent, about 5 minutes. Stir in remaining ingredients. Heat to boiling, reduce heat to low. Simmer uncovered, about 10 minutes, stirring occasionally. Makes about 2 1/3 cups of sauce.

Peach BBQ Sauce

1 can (16 oz.) **Peaches**, drained
1/2 cup **Brown Sugar**
1/2 cup **Ketchup**
1/3 cup **Vinegar**
2 tbsp. **Soy Sauce**
2 cloves **Garlic**, chopped
2 1/2 tsps. chopped fresh **Gingerroot**
Salt and **Pepper**, to taste

Combine all ingredients and salt and pepper to taste in a blender. Purée until smooth.

Peanut Butter BBQ Sauce

1 medium **Onion**
3 cloves **Garlic**
3 tbsp. **Peanut Oil**
1 1/2 cups creamy **Peanut Butter**
1/2 cup **Brown Sugar**
1/4 cup **Lemon Juice**
1/4 cup **Soy Sauce**
1/4 cup **Worcestershire Sauce**
1/2 cup **Beer**
Tabasco® **Sauce** to taste

Process onion and garlic until almost liquid in food processor. Add peanut oil, peanut butter, brown sugar and process until smooth. Place mixture in a large mixing bowl and add balance of ingredients. Stir until well blended. An excellent marinade and/or basting sauce for ribs, pork or chicken. Makes 4 cups sauce.

El Paso BBQ Sauce

1 cup **Ketchup**
1/2 cup **Cider Vinegar**
1 1/4 tsp. **Sugar**
1 1/4 tsp. **Chili Powder**
1/8 tsp. **Salt**
1 1/2 cups **Water**
2 stalks **Celery**, chopped
3 **Bay Leaves**
1 clove **Garlic**
2 tbsp. chopped **Onion**
4 tbsp. **Butter**
4 tbsp. **Worcestershire Sauce**
3/4 tsp. **Paprika**
Dash **Black Pepper**

Combine all the ingredients
and bring to a boil. Simmer
about 15 minutes. Remove
from heat and strain.

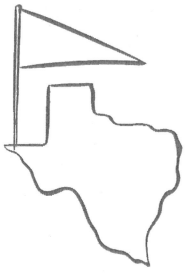

Asian BBQ Sauce

1 **Onion,** chopped
2 cups **Orange Juice**
4 cups **Ketchup**
1/2 cup fresh **Lime Juice**
1/4 cup **Cider Vinegar**
1/4 cup **Brown Sugar**
1 tbsp. **Salt**
1 tbsp. **Black Pepper**
2 tbsp. **Dry Mustard**
2 tbsp. crushed **Red Pepper**
2 tsp. **Garlic Powder**
1 tsp. **Chili Powder**
2 tbsp. **Tabasco**® **Sauce**
2 tbsp. **Tamarind Paste,** available at
    Indian and Asian groceries
2 tbsp. **Honey**
2 1/2 sticks **Butter**

Combine onion and 1 cup orange juice in blender. Puree until smooth. Transfer to medium size sauce pan and add remaining ingredients. Bring to boil then simmer 25-30 minutes. Cool; store sauce in refrigerator to up to 2 weeks.

Brown Sugar Rib Sauce

1 cup **Water**
1/2 cup **Brown Sugar**
1/4 cup **Worcestershire Sauce**
1/4 cup **White Vinegar**
1 tsp. **Chili Powder**
1 tsp. **Salt**
1/8 tsp. **Pepper**
1 tbsp. **Celery Salt**
Tabasco® Sauce few drops

Mix all ingredients together; stir over medium heat until boiling.

Teriyaki Barbecue Sauce

1/2 cup **Teriyaki Sauce**
1/3 cup **Apricot-Pineapple Preserves**
1/2 tsp. **Ginger Powder**
1/8 tsp. **Garlic Powder**
1 tbsp. **Cornstarch**
1/4 cup **Water**

Combine first four ingredients in saucepan and bring to a boil slowly. Combine cornstarch and water and add to sauce. Cook sauce until it thickens. Makes 1 cup.

Mama Vi's Family BBQ Sauce

1 cup **Honey**
1/2 cup chopped **Onion**
1 cup **Pineapple Juice**
1 small can **Pineapple**, crushed
2/3 cup **Red Wine Vinegar**
1 tbsp. **Salt**
2 tbsp. **Soy Sauce**
2 tbsp. **Ginger Powder**
1 tbsp. ground **Coriander**
4 large or 6 small cloves **Garlic**, minced

Combine all ingredients; cook over medium heat for approximately 40-45 minutes, stirring occasionally. Remove from heat; let cool. Apply to favorite meat or fish.

Aunt Evie's BBQ Sauce

1 tbsp. **Dry Mustard**
2 tbsp. **Brown Sugar**
2 tbsp. **Chili Sauce** or **Ketchup**
1/4 cup **Vinegar**
14 cup **Water**

Blend ingredients and heat over medium heat for 30 minutes.
Let cool and apply to meat.

Kumquat BBQ Sauce

1 cup **Tomato Juice**
1/2 tsp. **Black Pepper**
1 clove **Garlic**, chopped fine
1/2 cup **Dark Brown Sugar**
1/2 tsp. **Thyme**
3/4 cup **Kumquat Puree**

Put all ingredients into saucepan. Simmer, covered, for 20
minutes or until sauce becomes thick.

Onion BBQ Sauce

1 envelope **Onion Soup Mix**, your preference
1/2 cup **Dark Brown Sugar**
1 tbsp. **Prepared Mustard**
1 small **Onion**, chopped
1 cup **Chili Sauce**
1/4 cup **Lemon Juice**
1 1/2 **Water**

Mix all ingredients together and cook over medium-low heat for 20 minutes. Makes 2 1/2 cups sauce. Can freeze unused portion.

Rubs & Mops

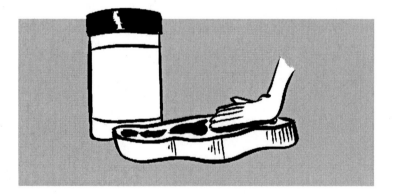

Hints about Mops:

- Meats should not soak for too long or they may become mushy and soft, especially seafood.

- Mop every 15 to 20 minutes when grilling for an hour.

- Mop every 4 to 5 hours when smoking for 20 hours or more.

- Use vinegar in the ingredients to enhance tenderness.

- Use water as a base to make a thin, mild mop.

- Use liquids such as Worcestershire sauce, fruit juices, wine or beer to enhance the flavor of meats.

Seasoning for Texas Barbecued Ribs

Mr. & Mrs. Johnnie Davis—Tallahasee, Florida

3 tbsp. **Salt**
3 tbsp. **Sugar**
1 1/4 tbsp. **Black Pepper**
1 1/2 tsp. **Paprika**
1 1/2 tsp. **Dry Lemon Powder** (unsweetened Kool-Aid®)

Mix together all dry seasoning ingredients and sprinkle ribs on both sides with mixture. Then baste with sauce.

Smoky BBQ Mop

1/2 cup **Liquid Smoke**
2 cups **Ketchup**
1/4 cup **Yellow Mustard**
2 tbsp. **Chili Powder**
1/4 tsp. **Celery Salt**
1/4 tsp. **Ground Oregano**
1 tsp. **Salt**

Combine liquid smoke, ketchup, mustard and chili powder in a blender and blend for one minute at slow speed. Add balance of ingredients and blend at medium speed until thoroughly mixed. Place sauce in a glass jar or bowl and refrigerate. Makes 2 3/4 cups.

BBQ Mop for Salmon

Barbecue Industry Association

1/4 cup **Butter,** melted
1 1/2 tsp. **Soy Sauce**
1 tbsp. **Lemon Juice**
1 tsp. **Worcestershire Sauce**
1 small clove **Garlic,** crushed
Dash **Tabasco**® **Sauce**
Liquid Smoke, few drops (optional)

Combine ingredients and mix well. Brush steaks generously with mixture. Place on oiled grill over hot coals. Grill, allowing 10 minutes per inch of thickness (or until salmon flakes easily with fork). Turn once halfway through cooking time. Baste frequently with marinade during cooking and once after taking salmon off grill. (Serves 4)

Tip: For ease in barbecuing, put salmon steaks between the two portions of a long-handled, hinged basket accessory and set basket on cooking grid. Make sure basket is well oiled to prevent steaks from sticking.

Spicy Dry Barbecue Mix

Cathy Allen—Capitola, California

1/4 tsp. dried **Oregano Leaves**
1/4 tsp. dried **Parsley Flakes**
1/2 cup mild **Mexican Chile Powder**
1/4 tsp. **Curry Powder**
1/4 tsp. **Dry Mustard**
1/4 tsp. **Onion Powder**
1/4 tsp. **Garlic Powder**
1/4 tsp. **White Pepper**
1/2 tsp. **Celery Salt**
Peanut Oil

Crush oregano leaves and parsley flakes finely between fingers. Mix all dry ingredients well together, and put in hand shaker. With a food brush, brush oil over the food to be barbecued. Generously sprinkle barbecue mix over oil; brush meat again to adhere. If continued coating is desired during barbecuing, stir some barbecue mix in with a little oil, and brush on. Barbecue mix should cover about six chickens, steaks, fish, etc.

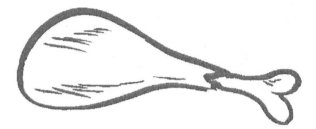

Dry Poultry Seasoning

Walter Jetton's LBJ Barbecue Cook Book
(Courtesy Simon & Schuster)

6 tbsp. **Salt**
3 tbsp. **Black Pepper**
2 tbsp. **MSG** (or other pep powder)
2 tbsp. **Garlic Powder**
2 tbsp. **Ground Bay Leaves**
1 tbsp. **Paprika**
2 tbsp. **Dry Mustard**

Sprinkle this on chicken and fowl before barbecuing. Makes about one pound of dry seasoning.

Merle's Mop

Merle Ellis—"The Butcher"
(Reprinted by permission of Chronicle Features, San Francisco)

1 cup **Vinegar,** cider or wine
5 tbsp. **Worcestershire Sauce**
2/3 cup **Salad Oil**
3 tbsp. **Butter**
1 **Lemon,** thinly sliced
2 to 3 cloves **Garlic,** minced
3 tbsp. grated fresh **Ginger**
2 tbsp. **Dry Mustard**

Combine all ingredients in a saucepan and heat until flavors are nicely blended. Use to baste any meat or poultry.

Louisiana BBQ Rub

2 tbsp. **Paprika**
2 tsps. **Garlic Powder**
1 1/2 tsps. dried **Thyme**
1 tsp. ground **Red Pepper**
3/4 tsp. dried **Oregano**
1/2 tsp. **Salt**
1/2 tsp. ground **Black Pepper**
1/4 tsp. ground **Nutmeg**

Combine all ingredients and store in an airtight container. Shake to blend before using.

Brisket Rub

Jane Kolb, Frisco, Texas

Can be prepared by the pound or by Tablespoon

1 lb. medium **Ground Pepper**
1 lb. **Ground Mustard**
1 lb. **Garlic Powder**
1 lb. **Light Chili Powder**
5 lbs. **Salt**

Mix all together and store in air tight container. Sprinkle liberally on both sides of brisket and rub it in.

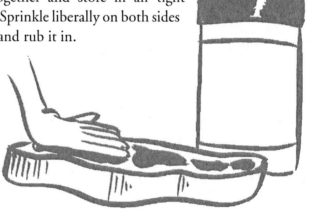

Mop for Barbecue Meats

Walter Jetton's LBJ Barbecue Cook Book
(Courtesy Simon & Schuster)

Use this mop to rub over meats or to baste them while cooking. The flavor will change and improve during use, for you are constantly transferring smoke and grease from the meats back to the mop concoction. Keep leftover mop refrigerated.

3 tbsp. **Salt**
3 tbsp. **Dry Mustard**
2 tbsp. **Garlic Powder**
1 tbsp. **Ground Bay Leaves**
2 tbsp. **Chili Powder**
3 tbsp. **Paprika**
2 tbsp. **Louisiana Hot Sauce**
2 pints **Worcestershire Sauce**
1 pint **Vinegar**
1 pint **Oil**
3 tbsp. **MSG** (or other pep powder)
4 quarts **Beef Stock**

Add all ingredients to beef stock and let stand overnight in refrigerator before using. Makes about 6 quarts of mop.

Southern BBQ Rub

2 tbsp. **Paprika**
1 tsp. **Salt**
1/2 tsp. **Pepper**
1/2 tsp. **Cayenne Pepper**
1/2 tsp. **Garlic Powder**

Combine all ingredients and store in a cool dry place. Use as needed for ribs, chicken and vegetables.

Tony's Best BBQ Rub

1 tsp. dried **Oregano**
1 tsp. **Onion Powder**
1 tsp. **Garlic Powder**
1 tsp. **Salt**
1 tsp. **Cornstarch**
1 tsp. freshly ground **Black Pepper**
1 tsp. **Beef-Flavored Bouillon Granules**
1 tsp. dried **Parsley Flakes**
1/2 tsp. ground **Cinnamon**
1/2 tsp. ground **Nutmeg**

Combine all ingredients and store in an airtight container.

Chipotle BBQ Rub

2 dried **Chipotle Peppers** (use 3 to heat it up a little)
3 tbsp. **Black Pepper**
2 tbsp. dried **Oregano**
1 tbsp. dried **Cilantro Leaves**
1 **Bay Leaf**
1 tsp. **Cumin**
1 tsp. **Onion Powder**
1 tsp. ground dry **Garlic**

Combine all ingredients in blender. Blend until finely ground. Store in an airtight jar. Can be stored in the freezer for up to 4 months. Great for brisket, steak, and pork.

Lemon-Rosemary Rub

1 1/2 tsp. grated **Lemon Peel**
1 tsp. crushed dried **Rosemary Leaves**
1/4 tsp. **Salt**
1/4 tsp. dried **Thyme Leaves**
1/4 tsp. coarse-ground **Black Pepper**
2 large cloves **Garlic**, minced

Combine all ingredients and use to season tender beef steaks or roasts. Makes enough to season 2 pounds of beef.

Southwestern Rub

1 1/2 tsp. **Chili Powder**
1 tsp. **Garlic Powder**
1/2 tsp. dried crushed **Oregano Leaves**
1/4 tsp. ground **Cumin**

Combine all ingredients. Use to season tender beef steaks or roasts. Makes enough to season two pounds of beef.

Note: Rubs are applied to the exterior surfaces of the meat just before grilling. They need no standing time. For convenience, rubs may be applied several hours in advance and the coated meat then refrigerated until grilling time. Flavors become more pronounced the longer the rub is on the meat. This recipe is courtesy of the National Live Stock and Meat Board.

Tip: Dry seasonings are rubbed on before grilling; marinades are used before and during cooking; sauces are brushed on just before cooking is completed.

Hickory Smoked BBQ Mop

1/3 cup **Worcestershire Sauce**
2 tbsp. **Tabasco® Sauce**
2 tbsp. **Red Hot Sauce**
4 tbsp. **Brown Sugar**
1/4 cup **Lemon Juice**
1/4 lb. **Margarine**
1 tbsp. **Prepared Mustard**
1 bottle (32 oz.) **Ketchup**
1 medium **Onion**, grated
1 tsp. **Barbecue Seasoning**
2 cloves **Garlic**, grated
1 cup **Hickory Smoked Barbecue Sauce**
Pinch of **Garlic Powder**

Combine all ingredients in a heavy saucepan and mix thoroughly. Cook for about 3/4 hour, stirring occasionally. Makes 2 quarts.

Sparerib Rub

2 tbsp. **Paprika**
2 tsp. **Seasoned Salt**
2 tsp. **Black Pepper**
2 tsp. **Garlic Powder**
1/2 tsp. **Cayenne Pepper**
1 tsp. **Oregano**
1 tsp. **Dry Mustard**
1 tsp. **Chili Powder**
1 tsp. **Thyme**
1 tsp. **Coriander**
2 tsp. cracked **Peppercorns**
1/2 tsp. **Allspice**

Combine all ingredients; mix to a fine texture. Hand rub this dry mixture onto washed and dried spareribs. Grill meat until done.

Can be used on other meats. Makes 1 cup.

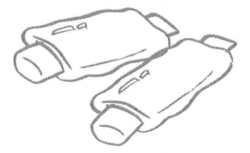

The All-American BBQ Mop

3 tbsp. **Olive Oil**

3 large **Onions**, chopped

1 can (28 oz.) **Tomato Puree**

3 cans (28 oz.) **Tomatoes with juice**

2 1/2 cups **White Vinegar**

4 tbsp. packed **Dark Brown Sugar**

4 tbsp. **Sugar**

1 3/4 tbsp. **Salt**

1 3/4 tbsp. freshly cracked **Black Pepper**

1 tbsp. **Paprika**

2 tbsp. **Chili Powder**

4 tbsp. **Molasses**

1 cup **Orange Juice**

1 tbsp. **Liquid Smoke**

8 tbsp. **Dijon-style Mustard**

Add oil to large saucepan; saute onion oven medium heat until golden brown. Add remaining ingredients and bring to a boil. Reduce heat to low and simmer, uncovered for approximately 4 hours. Cool and store in air-tight container. Refrigerate until use.

BBQ Joe's Meat Mop

1 cup **Beef Stock**
1/2 cup **Beer**
1/3 cup **Worcestershire Sauce**
1/4 cup **Vegetable Oil**
1/2 tsp. **Salt**
1/2 tsp. **Paprika**
1/2 tsp. **Dry Mustard**
1/2 tsp. **Black Pepper**
1/2 tsp. **Cayenne Pepper**
1/2 tsp. **Tabasco® Sauce**
1/2 tsp. **Garlic Powder**

Combine all ingredients in bowl and mix thoroughly. Use immediately or store in the refrigerator. Good for several weeks.

Southern Rub for Pork Chops

1 tbsp. **Garlic Powder**
1 1/2 tsp. **Cajun Seasoning**
1 1/2 tsp. **Salt**
1 1/2 tsp. **Italian Seasoning**
3/4 tsp. freshly ground **Black Pepper**
3/4 tsp. **Onion Powder**
3/4 tsp. **Barbecue Seasoning**
1/2 cup **Fruit Wine** of choice
3/4 cup **Honey**

Mix dry ingredients together. Rub on meat of choice. Pork Chops do very well. Next, mix wine and honey together to create a syrup. Use often as a baste.

Basic Rub for Ribs

1/2 cup **Dark Brown Sugar**
1/4 cup **Paprika**
1 tbsp. **Salt**
1 tbsp. **Black Pepper**
1/2 tbsp. **Cayenne Pepper**
3/4 tbsp. **Garlic Powder**
1 tbsp. **Onion Powder**

Mix all ingredients together to create a basic rub for spareribs.
Adjust the amount of cayenne pepper to suit your palate.

Marinades

All Purpose Game Marinade

Barbara Smith—Fort Worth

1/2 cup **Oil**
1 1/2 cups **White Vinegar**
1/4 tsp. **Liquid Smoke**
1 **Bay Leaf**
1/2 tsp. **Salt**
6 tbsp. **Worcestershire Sauce**
1 tsp. **Peppercorns**

Combine all ingredients. Refrigerate well before using. Good for dry cuts of game such as flank steaks, small game with little fat or round steaks. Makes 2 cups.

Southwestern Marinade

1/4 cup **Salsa**
2 tbsp. chopped fresh **Cilantro**
2 tbsp. fresh **Lime Juice**
1 tbsp. **Vegetable Oil**
1 clove **Garlic**, minced
1/4 tsp. ground **Cumin**

Mix all ingredients, stirring until well blended. Marinate in the refrigerator. Allow about 1/2 cup marinade for each 1 lb-2 lb of meat.

Basic BBQ Marinade

1/2 cup chopped **Onions**
1 1/2 tbsp. **Brown Sugar**
1 tbsp. **Vegetable Oil**
1/3 cup **Cider Vinegar**
1/3 cup **Ketchup**
1 tbsp. **Prepared Horseradish**
1 tbsp. **Water**
1/2 tsp. coarsely ground **Black Pepper**

Cook onion and brown sugar in a small saucepan over medium heat about 3 minutes or until onion is tender. Add remaining ingredients and continue cooking over medium heat 3-4 minutes, stirring occasionally. Remove from heat and cool thoroughly before adding to meat or poultry.

Remember to always marinate in the refrigerator. Allow about 1/2 cup marinade for each 1-2 pounds of meat. Turn meat occasionally during marinating so that all sides are equally exposed to the marinade. For flavor only, marinate 15 minutes or as long as 2 hours. For tenderizing, allow at least 6 hours.

Remaining marinade may be brushed on the meat during grilling, or used as a sauce, provided it is brought to a rolling boil for at least one minute prior to serving. Makes about 3/4 cup.

Simple Meat Marinade #1

1/4 cup plus 2 tbsp. **Olive Oil**
1/4 cup plus 2 tbsp. **Balsamic Vinegar**

Combine both ingredients, stirring until well blended. Remember to always marinate meats in the refrigerator.

Simple Meat Marinade #2

3 tbsp. **White Wine**
3 tbsp. **Olive Oil**
2 tbsp. finely chopped **Shallots**
2 tsps. **Fresh Herbs** (**Dill** or **Tarragon**)

Combine all ingredients. Stir well until blended. Marinate in the refrigerator.

Spicy Sparerib Marinade

Barbara Thomas—Olltewah, Tennessee

1 envelope **Dry Onion Soup Mix**
1 1/2 cups **Water**
1/3 cup **Honey**
1/4 cup **Soy Sauce**
2 tbsp. **Sherry**
1 tbsp. **Sugar**
1 clove **Garlic**, minced
1 tsp. **Ginger Powder**

Mix ingredients in large bowl. Add ribs and marinate two hours, turning often. Preheat oven to 350 degrees. Put ribs on rack in shallow roasting pan. Roast 1 1/4 hours or until tender. Turn and baste several times with marinade.

Pomegranate Meat Marinade

2 cups **Pomegranate Syrup**
1/4 cup **Olive Oil**
1 tbsp. **Lemon Juice**
1 1/2 tsps. **Salt**
1/4 tsp. **Pepper**
2 cloves **Garlic,** minced or pressed

Combine all ingredients into a large bowl. Stir until well-blended. Cover and refrigerate. Add meat and marinate, covered, for 4 hours.

Orange Marinade

1 cup **Mayonnaise-type Salad Dressing**
1/2 cup **Orange Juice**
2 tbsp. **Brown Sugar**

Combine all ingredients until well-blended. Cover until ready to use. Marinade meat in mixture for 1-2 hours in refrigerator. Grill and baste marinade. Discard unused portion.

Home-Style Steak Marinade

1 cup **Ketchup**
1/2 cup **Dry Red Wine**
1/4 cup **Vegetable Oil**
2 tbsp. **Wine Vinegar**
1 tsp. **Worcestershire Sauce**
1 tbsp. cooked minced **Onion**
1 clove **Garlic**, minced
1-1/2 lbs. **Flank Steak**, or other London broil

Combine all ingredients into large bowl. Store in air tight container. Refrigerate until ready to use. Place meat in a shallow baking dish. Pour mixture over steak, cover and refrigerate for 3 hours. Turn every hour.

Wine and Garlic Marinade

1 cup of **Dry Red Wine**
2 tbsp. **Red Wine Vinegar**
2 tbsp. **Olive Oil**
2 cloves **Garlic**, minced
1 tbsp. minced **Rosemary** or crumbled **Rosemary**

Combine all ingredients in a small bowl. Marinate beef or lamb in the mixture for at least 4 hours or overnight before grilling. Makes about 1 1/4 cups enough for 4 to 6 servings of meat.

Tip: Grill over Mesquite or Pecan wood

Spicy Seafood Marinade

1 cup fresh **Orange Juice**
1/4 cup fresh **Lime Juice**
2 tsp. **Oregano**
1 tsp. ground **Cumin**
6 canned **Chipotle Chilies**, minced
2 tbsp. **Wine Vinegar**
4 cloves **Garlic**
1 tsp. **Salt**
1 tsp. freshly grated **Orange Rind**
1 tsp. **Black Pepper**

Combine the orange juice and lime juice in a small saucepan and boil until reduced to 1/2 cup. Place juice and remaining ingredients into blender and blend thoroughly. If the marinade is to thick, thin with additional wine vinegar. Marinate seafood for 2 hours, poultry for 4 to 8 hours and meat overnight, turning a couple of times. Drain and barbecue normally.

Lime Marinade for Flank Steak

1/4 cup **Salad Oil**
1/3 tsp. **Lime Zest**
1/3 cup **Lime Juice**
2 cloves **Garlic**, minced or pressed
1 fresh **Jalapeno Pepper**, seeded and minced
1/2 tsp. **Cracked Pepper**

Mix together all ingredients in a small bowl. Pour over 1-2 pounds of Flank Steak, making sure meat is covered. Refrigerate for 4 hours or overnight.

Remove meat from marinade; place on grill and cook. Add Mesquite Wood for extra flavoring. Use remaining marinade to baste your steaks.

Horseradish Meat Marinade

2 cloves **Garlic**
2 1/2 tbsp. **Prepared Mustard**
1 tbsp. **Horseradish Sauce**
1/2 cup **Tomato Sauce**

Crush, peel and mash garlic cloves. Mix garlic, mustard, horseradish and tomato sauces together in a bowl or plastic bag. Add the meat to the marinade sauce and coat thoroughly. Cover and marinate for 2 hours or overnight in the refrigerator. Remove from marinade and cook.

Marinade is good for 1 pound of beef, lamb, pork or chicken.

Flank Steak Marinade

John Flynn, Colorado Springs, Colorado

1/3 cup **Soy Sauce**
3 tbsp. **Red Wine**
2 tbsp. **Lemon Juice** (frozen works)
1 tbsp. minced **Onion**
1/8 tsp. **Garlic Powder**
1/2 tsp. **Ginger Powder**

Marinate at least 4 hours in refrigerator, turning frequently. Grill as preferred.

Teriyaki Meat Marinade

1 1/2 cup **Soy Sauce**
1/2 tsp. **Onion Powder**
1/2 cup **Brown Sugar**
2 1/2 tbsp. **Lemon Juice**
1/4 tsp. **Garlic Powder**
1 tsp. **Ginger Powder**

Combine all ingredients in a bowl. Mix until dissolved and smooth. Let stand at least one hour to allow flavors to blend. Pour over beef, steak, pork, chicken, or fish and let marinate for at least two hours.

When Grilling: Use reserve marinade for basting. Brush meat, fish or fowl two or three times while cooking. This works excellent on shish-kebabs as well.

Teriyaki

Lamb Chops Marinade

2/3 cup **Apple Juice**
1/2 tbsp. **Curry Powder**
1/2 tbsp. **Ground Cumin**
1/4 tbsp. **Garlic Powder**

Combine all ingredients in bowl. Add lamb chops and cover completely. Marinade chops for 8 hours. Grill over Pecan wood for a distinct flavor.

Fish Marinade
a la Orange

1 cup **Dry White Wine**
2 tbsp. **White Vermouth**
2 tbsp. **Olive Oil**
1 tsp. dried **Rosemary**
1/2 tsp. ground **Black Pepper**
Grated Zest of 1 **Orange**

Combine all ingredients and marinate fish at least one hour before grilling.

Marinated Pork Tenderloin

John Flynn, Colorado Springs, Colorado

1/2 cup **Peanut Oil**
1/4 cup **Hoisin Sauce**
1/4 cup **Soy Sauce**
1/2 cup **Rice White Vinegar**
1/4 cup **Dry Sherry**
1/2 tsp. **Hot Chili Oil** (optional)
1 tbsp. **Dark Sesame Oil**
4 **Green Onions**, chopped
4 cloves **Garlic**, minced
2 tbsp. minced fresh **Ginger**
2-4 **Pork Tenderloins** (3 lbs. total)

Note: You can substitute Gilroy Farms products for fresh garlic and ginger. The bottles have amounts to substitute.

Combine ingredients and pour over meat. Marinate 3-4 hours at room temperature or for a longer time in the refrigerator. Grill over medium hot coals for 9-11 minutes per side.

Neither Snow nor Rain… (or even dark of night) stops John Flynn from grilling. He grills year-round in the foothills of the Rocky Mountains to the delight of family and friends. Snowstorm? That's what the earmuffs, gloves and galoshes are for!

Chicken Marinade

1/4 cup **Water**
1/2 cup **Olive Oil**
1/2 cup **Wine Vinegar** or **Lemon Juice**
2 tsp. **Salt**
1/4 tsp. **Pepper**
1 tsp. **Paprika**
1 tbsp. **Sugar**
1 tsp. **Garlic Salt**
1 tsp. minced **Onion**

Combine ingredients; stir until well blended. Let stand 60 minutes. Marinate chicken for at least one hour in the refrigerator before cooking.

Mom's Steak Marinade

1 tbsp. minced **Onion**
2 tsp. crushed **Thyme**
1 tsp. **Marjoram**
1 **Bay Leaf**, crushed
1 cup **Wine Vinegar**
1/2 cup **Olive Oil**
3 tbsp. **Lemon Juice**

Combine all ingredients until well mixed. Bring to boiling over medium heat. Reduce to simmer for 10 minutes. Cool. Refrigerate until ready to use.

Home-Grown Ham Marinade

2 cup **Brown Sugar**
2 cup **Wine Vinegar**
2 cup **Water**
1 large **Onion**, chopped
2 cup **Beef Consommé**
1 tsp. **Mustard Seed**
1/2 tsp. **Celery Seed**
1/2 tsp. cracked **Pepper**
2 cloves **Garlic**, minced

Add all ingredients to medium-size sauce pan. Bring to boil; reduce heat and simmer for 15 minutes.

Fred's Teriyaki Flank Steak Marinade

1/2 cup **Soy Sauce**
3 tbsp. **Honey**
2 tbsp. **Vinegar**
1 1/2 tsp. **Ginger Powder**
1/4 cup **Olive Oil** (or oil of preference)
2 cloves **Garlic**, crushed
4 **Green Onions**, chopped

Combine all ingredients. Refrigerate. When ready to use, Marinate flank steak overnight. Grill following day.

Coffee Marinade

1/2 cup **Coffee,** decaf or regular
2 tbsp. **Sesame Oil**
1/2 cup **Soy Sauce**
1/2 tsp. **Salt**
1/2 tsp. **Garlic Powder**

Mix all ingredients together. Stir well. Can use immediately or store in refrigerator until ready. For best results, marinate meats for 8 to 12 hours.

Index

O

P

R

Rubs and Mops

S

Sauces

Recipe:_____

From:_____

Ingredients:

_____   _____

_____   _____

_____   _____

_____   _____

_____   _____

Directions:_____

_____

_____

_____

_____

Recipe:_____

From:_____

Ingredients:

_____   _____

_____   _____

_____   _____

_____   _____

_____   _____

Directions:_____

_____

_____

_____

Cookbooks USA
• For Cookbook Lovers of all ages! •

Have you been to the ultimate cooking website yet?!

At **Cookbooks USA** you'll find a cookbook for every occasion and palate. Over 20 recipe categories to choose from and enjoy. BBQ, Desserts, Famous Chefs, Holidays, Regional and Southwestern are just a few.

But **Cookbooks USA** is more than cookbooks! It's food fun, with Celebrity Cookbook Reviews, Weird & Wacky recipes, Community Food Events and best of all, the first ever **Cookbook-A-Month Gift Package Program**! No club to join or extra books to buy – just great cooking with a new cookbook delivered to your doorstep every month. What a terrific gift!

You'll even find grandma back in the kitchen with the *"Grandma's Favorite ..."* series.

From free recipes to Fundraising with Cookbooks and a *Fun, Friendly & Free Monthly Foodletter*, discover a whole new world of cooking and food enjoyment at **Cookbooks USA.**

Mmmmmm! Good things are cookin' at

www.cookbooksusa.com

If you love cookbooks, then you'll love these too!

GOLDEN WEST ☼ PUBLISHERS

More than 180 recipes for salsa, dips, salads, appetizers and more!
$9.95

Make your favorite Mexican dishes in record time! Excellent tacos, tostadas, enchiladas and more!
$9.95

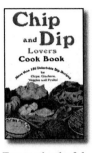

Easy and colorful recipes from Southwestern salsas to quick appetizer dips!
$9.95

Celebrate the tortilla with more than 100 easy recipes for breakfast, lunch, dinner, and desserts!
$9.95

More than 200 "wild" recipes for large and small game, wild fowl and fish.
$9.95

A collection of authentic Arizona recipes. Including Indian, Mexican, and Western foods.
$9.95

This unique book explores the age-old recipes that are rich with the heritage of New Mexico.
$9.95

Easy recipes for the traveling cook. Over 200 recipes to make in your RV, camper, or houseboat.
$9.95

Prize-winning recipes for chili, with or without beans. Plus taste-tempting foods made with flavorful chile peppers.
$9.95

What's more American than eating apple pie? Over 150 favorite recipes for appetizers, main and side dishes, pies, beverages, and preserves.
$9.95

Over 175 recipes for soups, breads, muffins, pies, cakes, cheesecakes, cookies, and even ice cream! Carving tips, trivia, and more.
$9.95

250 authentic, home-style recipes for tacos, tamales, menudo, enchiladas, burros, salsas, chile rellenos, guacamole, and more!
$9.95

www.goldenwestpublishers.com